The Real Estate Investment Pocket Guide

Key Concepts for Understanding
Real Estate Programs

Authored by:
Alan J. Parisse, SRS
and
Richard G. Wollack, SRS
with
Joyce G. Harold

Publisher:
Consolidated Capital Communications Group, Inc.
Emeryville, California

The Real Estate Investment Pocket Guide

Key Concepts for Understanding
Real Estate Programs

Publisher:

Consolidated Capital Communications Group, Inc.
publishers of:

Tax-Advantaged Investments
The Digest of Financial Planning Ideas
and other services for the investment community

Published by Consolidated Capital Communications Group, Inc.
1900 Powell Street, Suite 1000, Emeryville, California 94608

ISBN 0-930032-03-9

Current Printing (Last Digit)
10 9 8 7 6 5 4 3 2

Library of Congress Cataloging in Publication Data
Parisse, Alan.
 The real estate investment pocket guide.
 Includes index.
 1. Real estate investment. I. Wollack, Richard G., 1945–   . II. Title.
HD1382.5.P37   1983   332.63'247   83-7418

Contents

Contents (cont'd)

Contents (cont'd)

Illustrations

Background: Why We Created The Real Estate Investment Pocket Guide

When we published the now widely used and comprehensive program on tax shelters, **Tax-Advantaged Investments (TAI)**, a year ago, something became increasingly apparent to us: TAI is a professional resource and educational tool for all types of tax-advantaged programs, but it only skims the top of the *tax-shelter* product the authors are understandably most partial to: real estate. Hence, **The Real Estate Investment Pocket Guide.**

Real estate—an investment vehicle all of you know at least a little about. And, no wonder you are comfortable with real estate: Chances are, you spend more of your income on real estate than on any other item. And, in the past decade, along with oil and gas *syndications*, real estate syndications have been at the top of the list in public dollars raised—money "pooled" from many investors to buy income properties, thus taking advantage of economies of scale, professional management, and diversification to maximize tax advantages and investment return.

We hope you'll agree that, although the scope of this guide is necessarily limited to real estate, we've successfully expanded on the real estate investing overview introduced by TAI and thus have produced another permanent reference for our industry.

Alan J. Parisse, SRS   Richard G. Wollack, SRS

Preface

The Real Estate Investment Pocket Guide answers
some of the most frequently asked questions about
income real estate for those interested in real estate
investment programs.

During the past decade, the short- and long-term
benefits of income real estate made real estate investment programs attractive to hundreds of thousands of
investors . . . in many cases, individual investors who
would not have had sufficient capital or expertise to
participate in the benefits of any substantial real estate
investment, as well as larger investors who needed professional sponsorship, management, and guidance in the
ownership of large properties.

For Investment Professionals or Professional Investors

You will find this real estate guide valuable if you are
an investor; an attorney, accountant, or business advisor
who has been asked to advise a client; or a securities rep-
resentative who is seeking the background to properly
and effectively present real estate investment programs
to clients or to their advisors. In other words, when
you've completed this guide, you should be able both to
evaluate real estate investment programs and to commu-
nicate the benefits of those programs to others.

Scope: Equity Investment in Multi-Family Programs

We've limited the guide's scope to the basics of equity
investing in multi-family properties—basics that even
many who have been in the real estate investment business for years at times forget. Even if you don't intend to
become an expert in real estate, you will find that this

(continued)

guide provides a working knowledge of equity real estate investment programs without overwhelming you with technical details.

Structure: Real Estate Investing Benefits, Vehicles, and Evaluation

We'll begin with an overview of real estate, then describe its benefits, financing and taxation techniques, valuation, and various investment vehicles. We will go on to provide an overview of the future of real estate investing as we see it, then we'll wrap up with a checklist for evaluating equity programs.

Question-and-Answer Format: Graphic Examples and Cross-References

The question-and-answer format simplifies and highlights key concepts. Throughout the text we include examples, illustrations, and graphics to further clarify and demystify this sometimes complex investment field.

For ease of reference, terms defined in the indexed glossary (beginning on page 74) are highlighted in the text.

THE AUTHORS

Benefits
of Real Estate

- What Makes Real Estate a Good Investment?
- What Are the Benefits of Investment Real Estate?

Q What makes real estate a good investment?

- **Fundamental Need**
- **Favorable Tax Treatment**
- **Inflation Hedge**
- **Limited Supply**
- **Expensive to Replace**

Real estate's importance to everyone is illustrated by the various segments of the real estate industry that are critical to our basic needs: food, shelter, and clothing. By housing the places where we live, work, shop, and play, real estate touches all of our lives. Its value, in part, lies in our attachment to (and dependence upon) land, residences, shopping centers, office complexes, recreational centers, warehouses, and public buildings.

Many find attractive the favorable treatment real estate receives under income tax laws. Also, our sophisticated monetary system has historically lent money on real estate at rates below inflation, making *leverage* relatively inexpensive. However, there is a more basic reason for real estate's appeal: Real estate is a limited resource that meets a fundamental human need . . . Its relative value is determined by supply and demand. And the simple fact is: They aren't making any more land.

These are some of the reasons why, as a general rule, real estate continues to rise in value over time. Add to these: government regulation, environmentalism, high financing costs, and general inflation, all of which have joined forces to drive up the costs of labor, materials, and buildable land.

"First, . . . lands are of permanent value; . . . there is . . . almost a certainty of their rising exceedingly in value; and secondly, . . . our paper currency has depreciated considerably, and . . . no human foresight can tell how low it will get. " George Washington

"Managed with reasonable care it is about the safest investment in the world. " Franklin D. Roosevelt

Q What are the benefits of investment real estate?

- Cash Distributions
- Tax Benefits
- Equity Build
- Appreciation

Investors in income-producing real estate can benefit in four different ways:

1. Cash Distributions

Successful income real estate will eventually, if not immediately, provide cash distributions from property operations. These cash distributions should increase over time.

2. Tax Benefits

Income real estate enjoys many tax benefits. At the inception of the investment, cash distributions are usually "sheltered," in whole or in part, from federal income taxes.

In addition, even a moderately *leveraged* real estate investment usually generates tax losses without a concurrent economic loss. These tax losses can shelter income from the property and from unrelated outside sources.

In addition, appreciation on real estate is normally taxed at the lower *capital gains* rates.

3. Equity Build/Loan Reduction

Increases in the investor's *equity* result from *principal payments* made on the loan(s) against the property. This loan *amortization* is considered a benefit because the property owner is paying off the loan with rent dollars supplied by the tenant.

4. Appreciation

Improvements to the property itself justify increased rental rates, generating more revenue. As a higher rent level is maintained, a higher selling price can be asked by the owner. Appreciation, of course, also results from changing market conditions and, indirectly, general inflation.

What Makes Real Estate Popular?

Tax & Financing Benefits of Real Estate

- What Are the Sources of Tax Benefits Available in Real Estate Programs?
- How Can Real Estate Generate a Cash Profit and Still Show a Tax Loss?
- What Is the Economic Effect of Cost Recovery Benefits?
- What Happens as the Investment Matures?
- What Is Leverage and How Does It Work?
- Can Leverage Ever Work Against an Investor?
- Who Makes Loans on Income Real Estate?
- Do Lenders Ever Take "A Piece of the Action"?
- Why Would a Seller Take a Note Instead of Cash?
- How Else Does a Seller Benefit by Taking Back a Loan?
- What Is a Wraparound Mortgage?
- Who Are the Buyers with Cash?

What are the sources of tax benefits available in real estate programs?

- Accelerated Cost Recovery System (or Depreciation)
- Maintenance Expense Deductions
- Capital Gains
- "Tax-Free" Refinancing

*What Are the Sources of the
Tax Benefits of Real Estate Programs?*

Real estate programs offer significant tax and income-sheltering benefits. These benefits are generally due to one or more of the following:

1. Straight-Line Depreciation or Accelerated Cost Recovery System (ACRS)

Depreciation and *ACRS* are accounting methods designed for tax purposes to allow for the gradual deduction of the cost of a capital asset over its *cost recovery* period. Cost recovery periods are defined by a property's "class," as set by law. Most real property is 15-year property.

Both depreciation and cost recovery deductions can enable real estate to simultaneously generate cash distributions and tax losses.

Straight-line depreciation allocates the cost of the asset equally over its cost recovery period; as an example, assume an investor purchased a building for $150,000 at the beginning of the year. The straight-line depreciation would be $10,000 per year ($150,000 cost divided by 15-year cost recovery period).

ACRS, on the other hand, allows larger deductions in the early years using tables provided by the Internal Revenue Service. However, this "acceleration" of deductions reduces the amounts of the later years' deductions and often results in additional taxes when the investor sells the property.

2. Deductibility of Maintenance Expenses

While the deductibility of maintenance expenses is not an unusual tax benefit, when combined with depreciation, it helps create excess tax losses. Not only can you deduct depreciation regardless of whether or not the building is actually losing value, you can also deduct maintenance costs, costs that perhaps even improve the value and sales potential of the building.

3. Capital Gains Treatment on Sale

As with other capital investments, real estate is generally eligible for the lower *capital gains* tax rates, if held for more than a year.

4."Tax-Free" Refinancing

At some point during the life cycle of a real estate investment, it is not uncommon for the higher income to justify refinancing—in other words, replacing the original loan with a new, and often larger, loan. A refinancing produces a cash distribution to the extent the new loan exceeds the remaining balance of the original loan. When no concurrent sale occurs, this cash is generally not subject to current taxation.

Q How can real estate generate a cash profit and still show a tax loss?

A unique feature of real estate is its ability to generate a positive cash flow "profit," protect that cash from tax, and, at the same time, produce "paper" tax losses that shelter taxable income from outside sources. In other words, not only does the cash from the property get into your pocket without tax, but, in addition, you report the tax losses to the IRS and in turn can reduce your taxable income from other sources.

Let's look at an example of a simple real estate transaction to explain this phenomenon.

How Real Estate Can Generate a Cash
Profit and Still Show a Tax Loss.

This cartoon illustrates the example on pages 12 through 15.

Example:
Assume we have a property from which we collect $20,000 per year in rent.

From this $20,000 effective gross income we pay, say, $8,000 in operating expenses (such things as utility bills, real estate taxes, insurance, maintenance costs, and the on-site manager, if any). That leaves us with $12,000, which is our "net operating income." Then, if our annual payments on the mortgage against the property totaled $11,000 (including interest and principal reduction), our remaining cash flow is $1,000. That's cash in our pocket of $1,000.

Despite a $1,000 cash flow "profit," we report a $7,500 loss to the IRS! (Note that, typically, there would be differences in the way "taxable income" and "operating expenses" would be reported on the two types of statements. However, for purposes of simplicity, we reflect no difference.)

Let's look at the differences between the two statements. The first major difference between the two statements occurs because of the tax treatment of debt payments. Although all loan payments naturally reduce cash flow, only the portion of the $11,000 debt service allocable to interest ($10,500 in our example) is allowable as a deduction on the tax statement. The $500 of the debt payment reducing the principal is not a tax-deductible expense.

Note that if we were to stop here, our statement would show a taxable profit. ($12,000 net operating income less $10,500 interest is a $1,500 profit.) Far from showing a profit, however, our tax statement shows a $7,500 loss.

CASH FLOW STATEMENT
First 12-Month Period

	$					
Gross Income	$	2	0	0	0	0
Less: Operating Expenses	(		8	0	0	0)
Net Operating Income		1	2	0	0	0
Less: Debt Payment	(	1	1	0	0	0)
Cash Flow	$		1	0	0	0

P & L STATEMENT FOR IRS: Same Building
First 12-Month Period

	$					
Gross Income	$	2	0	0	0	0
Less: Operating Expenses	(		8	0	0	0)
Net Operating Income		1	2	0	0	0
Less: Interest on Debt	(	1	0	5	0	0)
Taxable Income before Cost Recovery			1	5	0	0
Less: Cost Recovery - Building	(		9	0	0	0)
Taxable Income (Loss)	$	(	7	5	0	0)

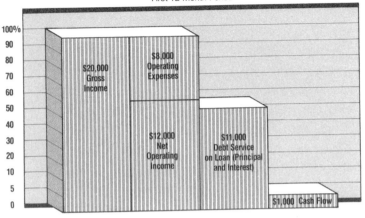

CASH FLOW STATEMENT
First 12-Month Period

- $20,000 Gross Income
- $8,000 Operating Expenses
- $12,000 Net Operating Income
- $11,000 Debt Service on Loan (Principal and Interest)
- $1,000 Cash Flow

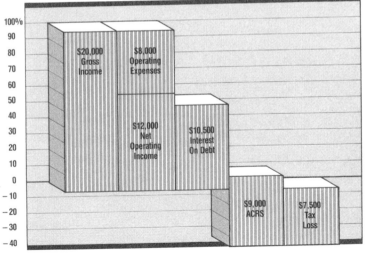

P & L STATEMENT FOR IRS: Same Building
First 12-Month Period

- $20,000 Gross Income
- $8,000 Operating Expenses
- $12,000 Net Operating Income
- $10,500 Interest On Debt
- $9,000 ACRS
- $7,500 Tax Loss

The *cost recovery* deductions create this tax shelter, because after we further deduct the $9,000 in cost recovery from our $1,500 taxable income, we show our $7,500 loss. (The $9,000 ACRS is arrived at by multiplying the cost of a building by a factor from a table published by the IRS. The factors vary based on the month of the year in which the property was purchased. An investor could also use straight-line depreciation.)

The $7,500 in our example is called a "paper" loss because the cost recovery deductions do not involve an expenditure of cash. The deductions are an allocation of the cost of a capital asset that, for tax purposes, is losing value. What makes the cost recovery deductions so attractive is that the real estate probably is not, in fact, losing value. On the contrary, it will most likely appreciate in value as time goes on.

It is also worth noting that *leverage* —the use of borrowed funds—increases the attractiveness of the cost recovery benefits. Why? Because cost recovery deductions are available on the full purchase price of the property, including the portion purchased with borrowed funds. In other words, an individual investor purchasing an income-producing property for say, a million dollars, receives the same cost recovery benefits without regard to whether his/her down payment was one dollar, $100,000, even $1,000,000. The larger the portion of the purchase price that is financed, the more the tax benefits are leveraged.

Q What is the economic effect of cost recovery benefits?

The tax-shelter umbrella on page 16 shows how cost recovery deductions are allocated. The umbrella consists of the $9,000 cost recovery benefit deducted in our example. The umbrella first shelters the $500 of the property's income that was allocated to *principal payments.* (Of the $11,000 debt payment, $10,500 was applied to deductible interest and $500 to non-deductible principal.) Since the $9,000 cost recovery deduction is $8,500 greater than the principal payments, the $8,500 is available to shelter the cash flow from the property ($1,000).

The excess of $7,500 ($8,500 − $1,000) is available to shelter income from other sources.

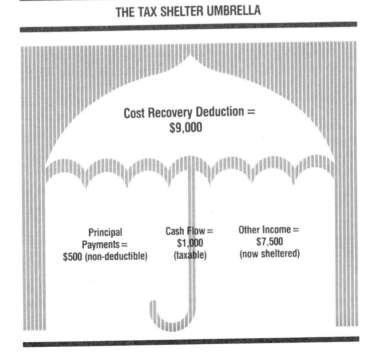

THE TAX SHELTER UMBRELLA

Cost Recovery Deduction = $9,000

Principal Payments = $500 (non-deductible)

Cash Flow = $1,000 (taxable)

Other Income = $7,500 (now sheltered)

Q What happens as the investment matures?

This very favorable circumstance does not go on forever. As the investment matures, the tax benefits decrease for one or more of the following reasons:

Increased Equity Build (Loan Amortization)

■ Generally, as a loan ages, the portion of the loan payment applied to principal increases, while the amount allocated to interest decreases. As a result, more and more of the cost recovery deduction is needed in order to shelter the increasing portion of the property's income that is allocated to principal payments. So, while the investor benefits by having his/her equity in the property (value less the loan balance) increase, the cost recovery deductions are being used up.

Increased Cash Flow

■ The cash flow generated by the property may well increase in the future. While this is clearly positive, it also has the effect of using up more of the cost recovery deductions.

Decreased Cost Recovery Deductions

■ With *ACRS*, the deductions diminish as time passes and, regardless of whether ACRS or straight-line *depreciation* is used, these deductions generally run out after 15 years of ownership.

Consequently, as time goes on, the excess (or over-throw) loss provided by ACRS benefits is reduced and eventually eliminated. At first, part of the cash flow becomes taxable. In time, all the cash flow becomes taxable. Eventually, ACRS will no longer be sufficient to shelter the principal payments on the mortgage. If the property is held long enough, the investors will ultimately receive what is known as *phantom income* (taxable income in excess of cash income).

What Happens to a Tax Shelter When an Investment Matures?

Q What is leverage and how does it work?

Leverage is the use of borrowed funds. It allows the investor to obtain a comparatively large investment with a relatively small cash outlay. The investor's return will be enhanced if the *after-tax* expense for borrowing the funds remains less than the after-tax return from the investment.

Leverage is effective in increasing the tax and appreciation benefits from a real estate investment because, regardless of the cash down payment, the investor receives the same appreciation and the same tax and ACRS benefits.

Example:
An investor has purchased a $100,000 property that appreciates $10,000 in the first year.

While the property's rate of appreciation is 10% ($10,000 appreciation divided by $100,000), the investor's true percentage benefit is a function of the amount of cash put in. If the investor bought the property for all cash, the return from appreciation remains 10%. If, however, the investor borrowed 80% and invested only $20,000, the appreciation benefit would be 50% ($10,000 appreciation divided by the $20,000 cash invested).

"But," you say, "that example assumes the debt was without cost." You are correct; however, remember that the leverage (i.e. financing cost) is usually paid from the cash generated by the property and enhances tax

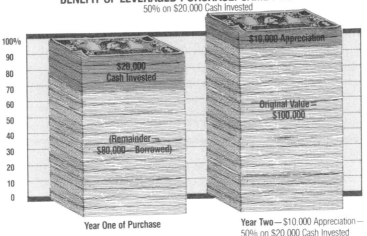

BENEFIT OF ALL-CASH PURCHASE: $100,000 PROPERTY
10% on $100,000 Cash Invested

$10,000 — Appreciation

$100,000
Cash
Invested

Original Value =
$100,000

100%
90
80
70
60
50
40
30
20
10
0

Year One of Purchase

Year Two—$10,000 Appreciation—
10% on $100,000 Cash Invested

BENEFIT OF LEVERAGED PURCHASE: SAME PROPERTY
50% on $20,000 Cash Invested

$10,000 Appreciation

$20,000
Cash Invested

Original Value =
$100,000

(Remainder—
$80,000 — Borrowed)

100%
90
80
70
60
50
40
30
20
10
0

Year One of Purchase

Year Two—$10,000 Appreciation—
50% on $20,000 Cash Invested

benefits as well because of the substantial interest deductions. But, certainly, the all-cash purchaser received a higher current cash flow.

*Leverage Will Push Up
Your Return . . .*

*But Too Much Leverage
Can Hurt You.*

Q Can leverage ever work against an investor?

Yes, leverage used imprudently can work against an investor. If the cost of the debt exceeds the total return from the property, negative or reverse leverage results. Remember, however, to compare not just the cash return but the total return before determining you have negative leverage. Total return includes cash distributions, tax benefits, equity build, and appreciation. In the worst case of negative leverage, the investor may not have enough cash flow to service the debt and risks foreclosure.

While the proper use of leverage maximizes returns, the risk of leverage can be hidden. The interest rate may be fine, and all the other terms may look great, but there may be a problem such as a *balloon payment* requiring the payment of principal at the end of, say, three years. In this case, the cost of the leverage could, in effect, be the loss of the property, because if the borrower cannot meet the balloon payment, the lender will be in a position to foreclose. Additionally, should cash generated by the property be less than that needed to service the debt, the likelihood of the owner losing the property by foreclosure also increases.

Q Who makes loans on income real estate?

The large property buyer/owner generally has three avenues of obtaining financing:

1. Traditional lending institutions such as banks, savings and loans, insurance companies, and pension funds;
2. Other entities such as *real estate investment trusts* and *real estate limited partnerships*, who often purchase existing loans; and
3. The property seller who takes back "paper" (a note) from the buyer rather than receiving cash upon property sale.

Who Makes the Loans?

Q Do lenders ever take "a piece of the action"?

Yes, traditional lending institutions, as well as real estate investment trusts and limited partnerships, are more and more structuring loans calling for "equity participation," or cash back from property operations, property sales, and refinancings. Such participation is an interest in the performance of the property securing the loan, and is sometimes known as a "kicker." With a participating loan, cash comes back to the lender when the property yields income above a defined level. This type of arrangement usually increases the overall return to the lending entity by enhancing its protection against inflation. In the end, the lender earns more than it would have with a conventional, fixed-rate mortgage. Thus, the participating loan is often structured at a base rate of interest below the current going market rate as a trade-off for the future equity in the property.

Q Why would a seller take a note instead of cash?

The answer varies by transaction and by seller. Sometimes a seller takes back paper simply because that is the only way to sell the property—there may not be a buyer who would pay sufficient cash to purchase with the existing mortgage. Often, however, the seller has determined that the return on investment will be increased by providing some or all of the financing required by the buyer. Why? In part, because the buyer may be willing to pay more for the property if he/she can leverage the tax and appreciation benefits by paying less cash down.

Everyone Wins When a Seller Takes Back Paper.

How else does a seller benefit by taking back a loan?

- **Wider Market**
- **Potential for Higher Yield**
- **Delayed Taxation**

A seller can actually be better off taking a portion of the price due him/her in the form of a note secured by the property being sold, also known as "taking back paper." The benefits are as follows:

- widens the market of potential buyers—the result is a faster sale at probably a higher price;

- increases potential for a higher yield on equity—for example, if the seller intends to put the cash in a money market fund, he/she might do much better by leaving some of the cash in a note and charging a higher rate to the buyer of the property; and

- delays taxes at sale—by electing an installment sale, the seller can delay taxes on sale until such time as funds are received. This is a two-fold positive effect: First, it tends to spread out the taxes due; second, it allows the full amount of the equity to earn interest, as opposed to taking the dollars out of the real estate, paying taxes on them, and then reinvesting what's left over.

A seller can increase his/her benefits even more by creating a *wraparound mortgage* (also known as "pur-chase money financing" or an "all-inclusive promissory note") in lieu of some or all of the cash.

What is a wraparound mortgage?

A wraparound mortgage (a "wrap") is, in essence, a larger loan that includes (or wraps around) a smaller loan. Perhaps the best way to define a wrap is by an example that explains one circumstance in which a wrap is appropriate.

Example:
First, let's assume a property is for sale under the following terms:

Price— $100,000
Existing first loan at 8.67% — $60,000
Seller's equity — $40,000

To assume the existing first loan, a new buyer needs $40,000 (40%) in cash to purchase the property ($100,000 price minus the existing $60,000 first loan). The buyer would then make payments totaling $5,200 per year on the first loan (assuming for simplicity the loan requires interest payments only).

The problem is that few buyers can put down 40%. As a consequence, the seller must do one of the following to sell the property:

1. Lower the price to attract a buyer with sufficient cash;

2. Obtain a new first loan; or

3. Take part of the $40,000 equity in the form of a new, second loan.

Wraparound Mortgage: The Seller Tailors the Loan To Fit the Buyer.

At first blush, it looks as though it's always best for the seller if the buyer gets a new loan from a third-party lending institution, such as a bank, and "cashes out" the seller. (And, indeed, many sellers would prefer this route as it avoids the risk of default on the loan by the buyer.) But the new loan usually would bear a much higher interest rate and annual payments that would, in turn, lower the return to the buyer. The buyer might then demand a lower price.

If, however, the seller wishes to retain the favorable first loan, the seller could "take back" a second loan on the property.

Example:

> Price — $100,000
> Existing first loan at 8.67% — $60,000
> Seller's second loan at 13% — $20,000
> Buyer's cash — $20,000

Assuming the going rate for a new first loan is 12%, the seller might charge a little more, say 13%, for the second loan. In this case, the seller receives $20,000 in cash and 13% on the $20,000 equity left in the project.

With a wrap, however, the seller could charge, say, 12% on the $80,000 wrap and receive a 22% effective annual yield on the $20,000 equity. How? Let's look at it.

Example:

> Price — $100,000
> Wraparound mortgage at 12% — $80,000
> (wrap includes $60,000 existing first loan)
> Buyer's cash — $20,000

By retaining responsibility for the $60,000 first loan and getting a note from the buyer for $80,000, the seller has an $80,000 asset, but is left with the obligation to pay the $60,000 loan. So the seller still has only the $20,000 equity (the $80,000 face amount of the wrap minus the $60,000 first loan).

On the $80,000 wrap, the seller would earn $9,600 (12% of $80,000). From this, the seller must pay $5,200 on the first loan, leaving a return of $4,400 ($9,600 minus $5,200), on the seller's $20,000 equity. Dividing the $4,400 net return by the $20,000 equity gives the seller a 22% per year return on equity.

So a primary advantage of a wrap is that the seller increases his/her yield from the sale. In addition, by leaving the equity in the project, the seller can delay tax on the sale. In our example, let's assume that the seller's gain equals his/her equity in the property ($40,000) and is eligible for *capital gains* treatment (taxed at a maximum effective rate of 20%).

DOLLAR YIELD TO SELLER

	All-Cash	Wraparound
Cash Received	$40000	$20000
Equity Left In	—0—	20000
Current Tax	(8000)	(4000)
Equity	32000	16000
Yield on Cash Received (at 12%)	3840	1920
Yield on Equity in Wrap	N/A	4400
Total Annual Yield on 40% Equity	$ 3840	$ 6320

If the seller sold the property for $100,000, all cash, all of the $40,000 equity would be subject to capital gains tax. A 20% tax on $40,000 is $8,000, leaving net equity of $32,000 (see "Dollar Yield to Seller" example). Let's assume the investor then puts the money into an investment earning 12%. $32,000 at 12% would yield $3,840. Now let's look at what happens if the seller were to leave $20,000 in equity in a wrap and take out only $20,000 in cash. The tax would be reduced from $8,000 (20% of $40,000) to $4,000 (20% of the $20,000 in cash taken out). At this point, the seller has two assets: (1) $16,000 in cash ($20,000 taken out minus $4,000 in tax) and (2) $20,000 equity in the note.

If we again assume the seller invests the cash at 12%, the $16,000 net *after-tax* cash received would generate a yield of $1,920. Added to that would be the $4,400 that the seller would receive on the $20,000 equity in the wrap. The total return is $6,320 ($1,920 plus $4,400). So by taking cash out, the seller receives a $3,840 yield. By leaving it in, the seller receives $6,320.

Q Who are the buyers with cash?

Mostly big institutions, but, surprisingly, the buyers also include small investors. You see, in large part, the buyers with cash are real estate investment programs organized by professional *sponsors*. These programs have been remarkably successful in attracting investment capital from a vast range of investors, including both the large institution and the small investor.

The sad thing is that many people will not participate in real estate investment programs primarily because the media often have had a tendency to focus only on the single-family-house market, depicting its volatility as risky and playing up those times when there is a seriously depressed real estate market. Unfortunately, most people assume that all types of real estate are questionable investments when the media produce such stories about the single-family-house market. The erroneous impression that conditions in the single-family-house market equate with conditions in the investment market (coupled with the average investor's tendency to buy at the peak and sell at the bottom) will keep many from investing at just the right time.

Valuation
of Real Estate

- How Do You Compute Replacement Cost?
- How Do You Use Market Data To Appraise a Property?
- What Are Two Income Analysis Approaches?
- How Do You Determine Value Using the Gross Multiplier Method?
- How Do You Determine Value Using the Cap Rate Method?

Appraisal of property is as much an art as a science. However, there are several primary methods in general use for determining the value of income real estate:

- **Replacement Cost Data**
- **Market Data (Sales Price Comparison)**
- **Income Analysis:**
  Gross Multiplier Approach
  Capitalization Rate ("Cap Rate") Approach

Q How do you compute replacement cost?

As a rule, *replacement cost* data gives you an idea of the upper limit of price you should pay for a property. Clearly, you should not pay more for a property than it would cost to replace it with an asset of equal earning power. To determine the cost of replacement:

1. Estimate the full cost of new, comparable construction;
2. Subtract the various forms of real, economic depreciation such as physical wear and tear, obsolescence; and
3. Take the net amount above (which is really the cost of replacing the asset with one of identical, long-term earning power) and add it to the value of the land.

How do you use market data to appraise a property?

Most frequently used in appraising single-family houses and land, the market data approach uses the prices paid for comparable properties:

1. Locate comparable properties that have recently been sold;
2. Contrast these "comparables" or "comps" with your subject property;
3. Make adjustments upward or downward in value of your subject property to allow for differences between it and the comps in regards to age, location, visibility, amenities, size; and
4. Draw a conclusion as to the value of your subject property.

3

Valuation
of Real
Estate

What are two income analysis approaches?

Rental income is, fundamentally, what creates value in investment real estate, so it makes sense to use an income approach to estimate or compare values by either a multiple of, or capitalization of, rental income. There are two forms of the income analysis: a simple form called the *gross multiplier* and a more sophisticated approach called the *capitalization rate* (or "cap rate") approach.

How do you determine value using the gross multiplier method?

The gross multiplier approach is a fairly straightforward method because it focuses on a property's revenue-generating capabilities. However, by focusing entirely on the property's rental income, this method does ignore differences in vacancies, operating expenses, utilities, property taxes, etc., as well as financing that may exist on the property and possible tax effects on various investors. Nonetheless, the gross multiplier works reasonably well in deriving a value close to actual value when comparing properties of the same type in similar markets, because, in the last analysis, it is largely the income-producing capabilities that determine a property's value.

To use this approach:

1. Use the market approach (described on page 35) to determine the sales prices of "comps";

2. Divide their individual sales prices by their annual gross rental incomes to achieve a "gross multiplier" factor;

3. Determine your property's anticipated annual income; and

4. Multiply your property's anticipated annual income by the "gross multiplier" to determine property value.

For most income properties, the marketplace regularly reflects a factor of between 5½ and 8½ times the annual gross rents. For properties where the tenants are responsible for their own utilities the gross multiplier factor tends to be higher. Although year by year and in different market areas, the factor fluctuates, a good rule of thumb is to assume a factor of 6 to 7½. In that case, a property generating $100,000 in annual gross rents would bring between $600,000 and $750,000 in most domestic markets. (See page 52 for a "value-added" example using the gross multiplier factor of 6.)

(See page 52 for a "value-added" example using the gross multiplier factor of 6.)

Q How do you determine value using the cap rate method?

Because it accounts for both income and expenses, the cap rate method is usually more precise than the gross multiplier method. Briefly, the primary steps in calculating cap rate are:

1. Estimate the annual gross income from the property;

2. Deduct an allowance for vacancies;

3. Deduct the annual operating expense to determine the annual "net operating income"; and

4. Divide the annual net operating income by the purchase price.

An investor who pays $600,000 for a property with an annual net operating income of $60,000 is experiencing a cap rate of 10%.

As you can see, the cap rate is expressed as a percentage and represents the current rate of return demanded by and in the market for a given type of property at a given time, assuming the property secures no financing (i.e., it is "free and clear"). Because the cap rate is influenced by many factors, it fluctuates from time to time. Given the market and the property in question, the basic factors used to determine cap rate are:

- Investor demand for the particular type of property
- Stability and level of estimated future income
- Risk related both to the type of investment and to the specific property
- Earnings and yields of alternative investments (adjusted for relative risk factors)

Basically, then, you can determine cap rates similarly to determining gross rent multipliers — by examining recent actual sales of similar properties in similar markets.

Example:
Assume a Property Has a Gross Income of $102,000, a Projected Vacancy of $4,000, and Operating Expenses of $38,000.

NET OPERATING INCOME

Following the steps outlined, we determine the net operating income of the property:

Scheduled Rents	$	102000
Less: Vacancy		(4000)
Gross Income		98000
Less: Operating Expenses		(38000)
Net Operating Income	#	60000

While projections of income and expense can be tricky, without doubt the most difficult step is determining the appropriate cap rate. Theoretically, the cap rate represents the rate of return investors are currently demanding from investments of similar risk and return. For now let's assume the cap rate for this property could be as low as 9% or as high as 12%, and we will look at the effect of changing cap rates on the estimate of value.

To determine what investors would be willing to pay for the property free and clear of any loans, we divide net operating income by the presumed cap rate of 9%.

We want to determine how much an investor demanding a 9% return would be willing to pay for the property. To make this determination, we divide $60,000 by 9%, and determine the value to be $666,667:

$60,000 divided by .09 = $666,667

Following the same method we see that assuming a 10% cap rate, the value is $600,000; at 11%, it is $545,455; and at 12% it is $500,000.

The more current return an investor insists upon, the less he/she is willing to pay. So—the higher the cap rate, the lower the value because a higher cap rate indicates buyers are demanding a higher return.

Also notice the rather wide differences in value that result from seemingly small changes in the cap rate. Thus, even a one-point increase in the cap rate has as much as a $66,667 decreasing effect on the value of a property in our examples. (See page 41.)

Income Analysis: The "Cap Rate" Method Accounts for Operating Expenses as well as Gross Income.

CAPITALIZATION RATE

9% CAP RATE	10% CAP RATE
$666,667 $60,000 9% CURRENT PROPERTY = NET OP. ÷ RETURN VALUE INCOME DEMANDED BY OWNER	$600,000 $60,000 10% CURRENT PROPERTY = NET OP. ÷ RETURN VALUE INCOME DEMANDED BY OWNER
11% CAP RATE	12% CAP RATE
$545,455 $60,000 11% CURRENT PROPERTY = NET OP. ÷ RETURN VALUE INCOME DEMANDED BY OWNER	$500,000 $60,000 12% CURRENT PROPERTY = NET OP. ÷ RETURN VALUE INCOME DEMANDED BY OWNER

3

Valuation
of Real
Estate

The cap rate approach assumes no financing—and financing, as we have seen in our examples of *leverage* and *equity* build, can have dramatic effects on value and investor return.

The Future
of Real Estate

- Why Do Properties Go Up in Value?
- What Is Inflation's Effect on Real Estate?
- What Other Trends Might Affect
  Real Estate Values?
- What Factors Specific to a Particular
  Property Affect Value?
- Is Investment Property Still a Good Investment?

4

The
Future
of Real
Estate

Q Why do properties go up in value?

A property may increase in value for a variety of reasons. There are, however, two broad categories of factors that affect value and, ultimately, an investor's return:

- **General Trends in Society**
- **Factors Having To Do with the Investment Itself**

Q What is inflation's effect on real estate?

Real estate investments benefit from most forms of inflation. To begin with, real estate typically is heavily reliant on borrowed money. Borrowers benefit from inflation, because they are able to repay their loans with cheaper dollars.

Inflation can also benefit a real estate investment by generally allowing owners to increase rents by amounts greater than expenses increase, disproportionately increasing cash flow. The reason: Rents start out higher than expenses, and the loan payments normally remain fixed. Let's look at an illustration.

If gross income and expenses increase at the same constant rate over time, the net operating income increases at a significantly higher rate. This effect is more significant if, as in our example, the property is subject to level loan payments. In our example, while the net operating income increased a total of an impressive 55% over only 9 years, the cash flow increased by more than 660%!

CASH FLOW STATEMENT

(In this case we will assume both income and expenses increase at the same rate, 5% per year, compounded.)

	Year 0	Year 1	Year 4	Year 9
Rents	$20000	$21000	$24310	$31026
Less: Operating Expenses	(8000)	(8400)	(9724)	(12410)
Net Operating Income	$12000	$12600	$14586	$18616
Less: Loan Payment	(11000)	(11000)	(11000)	(11000)
Cash Flow	$ 1000	$ 1600	$ 3586	$ 7616

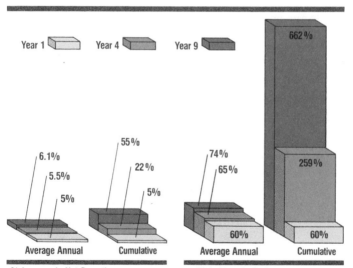

Year 1 ▭   Year 4 ▭   Year 9 ▭

% Increase in Net Operating
Income Since Year of Purchase ($12,000)

Average Annual — 6.1%, 5.5%, 5%
Cumulative — 55%, 22%, 5%

% Increase in Cash
Flow Since Year of Purchase ($1,000)

Average Annual — 74%, 65%, 60%
Cumulative — 662%, 259%, 60%

Remember, the value of investment property is always a function of the income it produces, so a dramatic increase in income should result in an equally dramatic increase in value.

■ What Happens If Inflation Stops?

A slowing of inflation would be a mixed bag for real estate investors. No doubt, there would be problems in some sectors of the real estate market. During the past decade, some investors purchased property (most particularly single-family homes) without regard to current economics.

In fact, many properties were purchased at prices that were totally dependent on inflation for the investor's return. If inflation declines substantially, these prices (and therefore any anticipated profit) would probably prove unrealistic.

On the other hand, a decrease in the rate of inflation will also have some positive effects on real estate values. Most important, a lowering of inflationary expectations will lower the interest rates.

■ How Will Lower Interest Rates Help Real Estate?

To begin with, lower interest rates imply lower *cap rates.* As discussed on pages 38 and 39, the lower the cap rate, the higher the property value. As shown, even a one-point decrease in cap rate has a great impact on property value. In our example, a decrease in cap rate from 10% to 9% has a $66,667 positive effect on property value.

For another thing, if lenders lock in today's high rates for a long term, anticipating a slowing of inflation, the new fixed rates will offer owners the ability to refinance expensive mortgages. Reducing *equity,* or debt service, would increase current cash flow profit (taking into effect the debt service paid).

■ Are There Potential Problems From Sustained Inflation?

The impact of inflation can be quite different when it continues over a period of years. To begin with, investors may overestimate future inflation and, as a result, "bid up" the price of properties beyond their value. In addition, developers and lenders may overbuild and create occupancy problems that could depress rents. Lastly, inflation makes lenders less willing to provide funds on terms attractive to the buyer. The result is a risky marketplace for the novice investor.

What other trends might affect real estate values?

- ■ **Population Trends**
- ■ **Housing Share of Income**
- ■ **Environmentalism**
- ■ **Technology**

- ■ **Energy**
- ■ **Replacement Costs**
- ■ **Lender Policies**
- ■ **Income Tax**

4

The Future of Real Estate

■ Population Trends and Household Formations

During the 1980s, three age groups (35 to 39 years, 40 to 49 years, and 65 years and over) should experience a tremendous increase. The first group contains the bulk of the first-time home buyers, while the second makes up the primary market for those trading up to larger and more expensive homes. The increase in the over-65 group indicates a demand for specialized housing. The trend towards smaller households will also increase the demand for apartment units.

SINGLE-FAMILY HOME MORTGAGE COSTS AS A PERCENTAGE OF "YOUNG FAMILY" INCOME 1974 and 1982

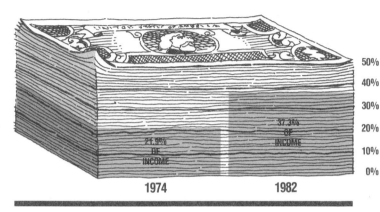

	50%
	40%
	30%
37.3% OF INCOME	20%
24.5% OF INCOME	10%
	0%
1974	**1982**

Source: Siff, Oakley & Marks (based on average income of families headed by individuals under 35 years of age—year of home purchase).

■ Share of Income Devoted to Housing

Inflation has pushed the cost of buying homes and renting commercial space well beyond traditional limits. In the future, Americans are expected to devote to housing a larger share of their income than ever before. The old rule of thumb (housing costs should equal 25% of income) is expected to rise to as much as 40% and, in fact already stands at more than 37% for young, first-time buyers. Businesses are making similar adjustments for commercial rents. These trends should have a significant upward impact on the share of income devoted to rents.

▪ Environmentalism

Although progress has been made against inappropriate environmental regulations, land investors must still account for the possibility that they may not be allowed to develop their land to its highest and best use (or even to develop it at all). The results are higher prices for buildable land and higher costs and risks for developers.

▪ Technology

Minicomputers and improved telecommunications will encourage many organizations to decentralize their office facilities. Business and government will no longer have so strong an incentive to remain in congested areas and can be expected to disperse into smaller locations. In addition, a growing number of persons will be able to work at home.

▪ Energy

While new technology will favor the suburbs at the expense of the cities, higher energy costs will favor the cities and mature suburban areas. In fact, energy availability and cost could drastically change the economics of many properties. For example, some existing buildings may become obsolete because they are not energy efficient.

4
The
Future
of Real
Estate

▪ Replacement Costs

As the cost of labor and materials goes up, the cost of replacing your property will also go up. That in itself will increase the value of the property, as a new investor would have to pay a significantly higher price to build a similar property.

■ **Lender Policies**

Lenders will continue to break away from their traditional roles. Many of them are likely to become increasingly involved in the full spectrum of real estate investment—everything from construction loans to equity ownership. As that trend occurs, more equity participation in refinancings, operations, and sales of properties probably will occur. (See pages 22-23.)

■ **Income Tax Law Changes**

Changes in tax laws and in rulings or interpretations can have a tremendous effect on the *after-tax* returns available from real estate investments and therefore on the value of the real estate itself.

Q What factors specific to a particular property affect value?

- ■ **Imperfect Marketplace**
- ■ **Selection**
- ■ **Management**
- ■ **Location**
- ■ **Alternative Use**
- ■ **Timing**

■ **Imperfect Marketplace**

As with the trends in society, there are innumerable factors affecting a specific investment's value. In fact, there are so many different influences on real estate value that it is considered an "imperfect" market. Unlike a consumer product on which there is sufficient homogeneity and information to create relatively balanced supply-and-demand, real estate exists in a heterogeneous, regionalized market on which there is often sketchy information. Because it is not a national market, the valuation and analysis of investment real estate relies on intangible variables. Thus, any attempt to structure rules, to predict "good" or "bad" times for sales or acquisitions is futile. We might say "there are no rules." Each property transaction is unique.

Below are some of the things to remember when you venture out into the relatively incalculable, diverse marketplace.

■ **Initial Selection**

Many a successful investor maintains that profits are made when you buy, not when you sell. By doing homework on the market, available financing, and cash and tax needs before acquiring a property, a knowledgeable investor can reduce risk and increase potential gain.

■ **Management**

The goal of good management is to enhance, as well as maintain, the value of an income property. Because the value is largely based on income flows, any fall-off in service to tenants or in the appearance of the property could reduce occupancy, impair income, and ultimately reduce its value.

4

The Future of Real Estate

With appropriate management capabilities and a marketing-oriented approach, undermanaged properties can provide attractive opportunities. Top-notch management can stabilize income by reducing turnovers and allowing for greater rent increases, which in turn attracts a higher quality resident, thus reducing risk of delinquency and eviction problems. By justifiably adding value through meaningful property improvements, quality managers can achieve all of the above.

Example:
Value-Added Property Management

Suppose a well-located and fundamentally sound property purchased on the best possible acquisition terms has been poorly managed and that the previous owner had been unable or unwilling to enhance the property's condition and therefore had sold it for something less than market value to a *real estate limited partnership.* The acquisition and management plan for the property might call for, among other things, new carpets in every residential unit at a cost of, say, $300 per unit. The average rent per unit might be increased $25 per month, producing an additional annual gross rental per unit of $300 ($25 × 12 months = $300). Thus, the cost of the carpet should be fully absorbed in 12 months, enhancing the quality of the unit, attracting quality residents who would not have rented the unit otherwise.

An even more important result is the increased market value of the property: For simplicity, we'll use the *gross multiplier* of 6, as discussed on page 37. When the property is sold, the $300 increased annual rental income increases value by about $1,800 ($300 × 6), on just that one apartment unit.

■ Location

Most everyone has heard the chime "location, location, location," and there is a lot of truth to it. But, what is a good location? Specific factors to look for include:

- ■ neighborhood
- ■ visibility
- ■ access
- ■ population base
- ■ area's economy
- ■ the political climate

- **Alternative Use**

In recent years, many investors have purchased income property to convert it to a different use. All sorts of conversions have taken place (i.e. hotels to apartments, apartments to hotels, office buildings to apartments, apartment buildings to offices, and so on). The most prevalent conversion has been to residential condominiums.

While a great deal of money has been made in the conversion business, legal complications, tenant complications, and market considerations should discourage the casual speculator. The primary risk to the converter is paying a premium price for a property on the assumption that it can be converted, and then finding out it can't.

- **Timing**

Last, but by no means least, is being there at the right time. Historically, real estate has followed a cyclical pattern, with different geographical areas at different stages of the cycle at the same time. This gives the national real estate investor an advantage in seeking out properties in areas that are at a favorable point in the cycle.

4

The Future of Real Estate

Q Is investment property still a good investment?

Yes. While there have been some well-publicized problems, particularly in single-family housing markets in the early 1980s, the basics that make investment real estate attractive are still very much in place. The Economic Recovery Tax Act of 1981 actually improved the tax benefits of real estate, and, in many respects, the underlying economics are better. In fact, the feeling in some quarters that "the bloom is off the rose" makes it just the right time to buy. The decline of long-term debt financing as we used to know it (the factor primarily responsible for many of the problems experienced in the single-family-house market) has created a buying opportunity for those with cash to make either high-equity direct real estate purchases or to pool their cash with other investors in group purchases.

Regardless of what happens in the home market, one thing is certain: A lot of money was made in investment real estate before the housing boom, and a lot of money will be made after the housing boom.

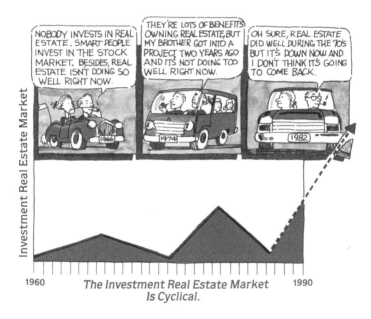

The Investment Real Estate Market Is Cyclical.

Investing in Real Estate Investment Vehicles

- What Is a Real Estate Syndication?

- Why Should I Invest in a Syndication, as Opposed To Buying on My Own?

- What Is a Limited Partnership?

- Are All Real Estate Programs Limited Partnerships?

- Why Are Limited Partnerships the Most Often Used Vehicle in Real Estate Programs?

- Are There Any Caveats Applying to Limited Partnerships?

- How Does a REIT Work?

- What Are Other Primary Differences Between a REIT and a Limited Partnership?

5

Investing in Real Estate Investment Vehicles

Now that we've covered most of the essentials to understanding investment real estate, let's take a look at how the average individual who does not care to shoulder the burdens of owning investment real estate can take a large piece of the real estate investment action via participation in a *syndication* with other investors.

Q | What is a real estate syndication?

A real estate syndication is a business organization that purchases one or more real estate investments. There are generally two types of participants in a syndication: the investors, who pool their money, and the syndicator, or *sponsor*, who manages the investment.

Typically, a syndication is organized as a *limited partnership*, wherein the investors are passive *limited partners*, and the syndicator is the *general partner*. As general partner, the syndicator is responsible for managing all the affairs of the partnership, including acquiring, managing, and eventually reselling the property. While the sponsor always has the ultimate responsibility for raising the capital from the investors, it may or may not directly approach investors. In fact, almost all major syndicators raise capital through unaffiliated securities firms (broker dealers).

Why should I invest in a syndication, as opposed to buying on my own?

- Access to Benefits
- Freedom from Management
- Professional Servicing

- Limited Liability
- Diversification
- Economies of Scale
- Staying Power

Why Should You Invest in a Syndication as Opposed To Buying on Your Own?

5
Investing
in Real
Estate
Investment
Vehicles

Investing in a syndication offers many advantages over investing in real estate directly:

■ Access to the Benefits of Real Estate

Many investors do not have sufficient capital to successfully invest in real estate on their own. Only a relatively small investment is required to participate in most syndications. Syndications can also provide a way to invest your IRA or Keogh plan in real estate. In fact, a number of offerings are set up specifically or exclusively to accept these types of investments.

■ Freedom from Management Burdens

Few dispute the financial attractiveness of investing in real estate. Buying income real estate individually, however, involves a significant commitment of time and may require that the investor have or develop substantial expertise in management. Another benefit of investing in a syndicate is that it allows for a passive investment. The sponsor is responsible for all the management, so the investor can concentrate on other business and personal interests.

■ Professional Management and Acquisition

Over time, syndicators should be able to perform better than individual investors. To begin with, the acquisition and management will be handled by a professional. In addition, by aggregating large sums of money, the syndicator can buy larger, generally more economically feasible, properties.

■ Limited Liability

If a syndicate is organized as a *limited partnership, real estate investment trust,* or corporation, the investor's liability will be limited, generally, to the amount of original investment. This is not the case with individual ownership, where the investor is fully liable for the debts of the investment.

- **Diversification**

Through syndication, an investor with as little as $1,000 can invest in a significant portfolio of properties that may vary by geography, type of property, financing arrangements, etc. Even those investors who do have the capital to make somewhat large individual investments rarely are able to reduce their risk by widely diversifying.

- **Economies of Scale**

Syndication also provides the investor with economies of scale—in other words, cost savings resulting from size. Purchasing more or larger properties can create certain cost savings. A simple example would be having one pool for a 20-unit apartment complex, versus only one for a 200-unit complex.

- **Staying Power**

Properly structured syndications provide staying power—the ability to make it through problems and downturns in the economy or the property. They do this in several ways:

- by raising extra capital and setting up a reserve for contingencies
- by diversifying into a number of properties in different geographical areas
- by avoiding unduly risky financing devices, such as short-term *balloon payments*

5

Investing in Real Estate Investment Vehicles

Q What is a limited partnership?

A limited partnership is a legal form of ownership. To be a valid legal entity a limited partnership must have at least one general partner and at least one limited partner. The partners normally execute a partnership agreement and record on the public record a summary of the agreement (called a Certificate of Limited Partnership).

Q Are all real estate programs limited partnerships?

No. Several other forms of ownership are used, including the *real estate investment trust* (REIT), the *general partnership*, and the *Sub-Chapter S Corporation*. While limited partnerships are by far the most commonly used form of ownership, depending on the objectives of the program, one of the other forms may be more appropriate. Since virtually all public real estate programs are either REITs or limited partnerships, we will restrict our discussion to these two vehicles, but primarily to limited partnerships, the most common type.

Why are limited partnerships the most often used vehicle in real estate programs?

- **Benefit Pass-Through**
- **Centralized Management**
- **Limited Liability**
- **Self-Liquidation**

The primary advantages of a limited partnership show the flexibility and attractiveness of the vehicle for investors:

- **Direct Pass-Through of Tax Benefits**

Unlike a corporation, the tax and economic benefits pass directly through the partnership to the limited partners. Not only can income be passed untaxed to the investors, but the investors also participate in their share of any tax losses. This benefit can be particularly important in real estate, because there are often significant tax losses during the early years of the investment.

- **Centralized Management**

The limited partners are free of the daily management.

- **Limited Liability for Limited Partners**

The limited partners are not personally liable for debts beyond the amount of their contributions to the partnership.

- **Self-Liquidation**

A *self-liquidation* feature is incorporated into nearly all limited partnership agreements. Self-liquidation simply means that as properties are sold and notes are eventually paid off, the money is distributed to the partners (usually within 10 years).

5

Investing
in Real
Estate
Investment
Vehicles

Q Are there any caveats applying to limited partnerships?

Yes. One "disadvantage" is restriction on transferability that is generally placed on investor interests (units). But this is mitigated by the self-liquidation feature discussed above. Restrictions on transfer are generally included in the partnership agreement to reduce the risk of the IRS holding your partnership to be, in effect, a corporation. While the risk of such an IRS ruling may be remote, if this were to occur, it would wipe out most of the partnership investor's inherent tax benefits.

In addition, an individual should analyze several other factors before making a limited partnership investment. For example, a potential limited partner should have sufficient asset liquidity in other investments (some say as much as one year's normal earnings).

Also, under the old maxim "Don't put all your eggs in one basket," an investor should be able to depend upon income from other sources in the eventuality that proceeds from one or more of the investments are lower than anticipated.

In most real estate limited partnerships, investors must meet minimum standards of income and net worth. Responsible investment sponsors recommend that potential investors consult with professional advisors to assess risks, objectives, and personal financial conditions.

How does a REIT work?

A REIT is a business trust managed by trustees. While somewhat like a mutual fund, the REIT invests in real estate mortgages or properties, rather than in stocks and bonds. So long as it meets the technical qualification requirements, a REIT has the tax advantage of being able to pass on its ordinary income to its investors (shareholders) without being first taxed at the trust level. While REITs do not enjoy the same tax treatment as partnerships, they do have their advantages. To begin with, REITs typically do not restrict transfers. (In fact, the shares of most trusts become traded securities.) Therefore, REITs do not have to self-liquidate. Another aspect of REITs is limited liability for all owners.

What are other primary differences between a REIT and a limited partnership?

Although it can shelter all its income, a REIT cannot pass excess tax losses through to its investors. While this could be a significant disadvantage, a REIT generally has investment objectives consistent with this limitation. For this reason, most REITs are structured to invest in mortgages, rather than ownership of real estate.

A REIT is restricted in the manner in which it carries on its business. For example, to avoid *double taxation* a REIT must distribute to shareholders at least 95% of its earnings. There are also various limitations on the types of investments a REIT may make.

Evaluation Checklist: Typical Equity Real Estate Program

- The Sponsor
- The Program
- The Properties
- The Property Management

6

Evaluation
Checklist

Now that we've covered the types of real estate investment vehicles available for income properties, let's take a look at a checklist to help you evaluate a sponsor, a program, its real estate, and its property manager.

Once you've completed the checklist, it's time to consult with your financial advisor, if you have not already done so, to help you determine how to proceed with the investment real estate program.

The Sponsor

Experience

_____ What is the sponsor's background in this type of vehicle?

_____ Is there continuity of management personnel?

_____ What is the general history of the sponsor's organization?

_____ Have previous programs been successful?

_____ What are:

        _____ the age of the organization?

        _____ net worth?

        _____ earnings?

        _____ growth pattern?

        _____ number of employees?

_____ Who are the decision-makers?

Financial/Fiduciary Abilities

_____ Does management have operational experience in:

    _____ acquisition of assets?

    _____ appraisal?

    _____ asset management?

    _____ liquidation of assets?

    _____ raising capital?

_____ What is the sponsor's track record regarding the frequency, amount, consistency, and sources of cash distributions?

_____ What banking relations does the issuer/sponsor maintain?

_____ What is the policy on cash reserves?

_____ Is management's compensation subordinated to, or dependent upon, the performance of the program?

Responsiveness

_____ What are the issuer's activities in:

    _____ internal audit procedures and investor financial reporting?

    _____ communications relative to tax data, asset acquisition and sales, and other significant events?

_____ How accessible is the sponsor's management?

6
Evaluation
Checklist

Reputation/Philosophy

_____ What is the sponsor's reputation within the industry?

_____ Has the sponsor ever been involved in investigations by the Securities and Exchange Commission, the National Association of Securities Dealers, Inc., or the states where it does business?

_____ Are all relevant risk factors and potential conflicts of interest disclosed and fully described in the offering material?

_____ What is the sponsor's investment attitude regarding:

    _____ single-tenant fad properties with limited use?

    _____ low-rent housing?

    _____ high-rent housing?

    _____ special-management properties such as hotels, motels, restaurants?

    _____ multi-tenant properties vs. single tenant commercial/industrial properties?

    _____ purchasing properties below replacement costs?

The Program

Structure

_____ Is there a provision for self-liquidation?

_____ Are potential risks and conflicts of interest disclosed?

Operations

_____ Have distributions and tax benefits been realized as originally anticipated in this program and in similar programs by the same sponsor?

_____ What percentage of the distributions has come from operations and what percentage from contributed capital?

_____ Are there regular reports to investors and to securities brokers?

The Properties

Diversification

_____ Is the program's portfolio geographically diversified so that it has holdings in more than one neighborhood, city, or region?

_____ Is the program's portfolio functionally diversified so that it owns more than one type of income property?

Acquisition/Sales Teams

_____ Who is responsible for selecting the properties for the program?

_____ Who is responsible for eventually selling the properties?

_____ What are their qualifications?

Track Record

_____ How well has management anticipated economic trends and conditions in selecting properties in previous programs?

_____ How long is the average holding period vs. that of competitive sponsors of similar programs?

_____ What is the sponsor's timing on the purchase of properties—identifying markets where rent increases were possible?

_____ What is the sponsor's timing on sale of properties —selling when market conditions are at the peak for a particular property in a given market?

Ownership Philosophy

_____ What is management's philosophy in adding value to properties with planned improvements?

_____ Is the sponsor willing to add value to the properties as judged necessary by the property manager during the holding period?

The Property Management

Experience

_____ Who is, or will be, managing the properties in the program?

_____ Is on-site staff adequate in number?

_____ Is administrative or home-office staff organized and up-to-date in management training and techniques?

_____ What is the manager's experience with properties in similar programs?

Abilities/Track Record

_____ Does the manager have experience in both high- and low-vacancy rental markets?

_____ What kinds of cash flows to investors have been produced by properties they have managed previously or are now managing?

_____ Do they have a proprietary attitude?

_____ Are they responsive to resident and tenant needs?

_____ Are their apartment rental practices and people marketing-oriented?

6
Evaluation
Checklist

Appendix

- Indexed Glossary
- Profiles
- Acknowledgements

INDEXED GLOSSARY

Definitions are cross-referenced to pages in the text where concepts are discussed in more detail.

Accelerated Cost Recovery A method for determining annual deductions on real estate and other capital assets that allows for larger deductions in the early years and for straight-line depreciation. See "Accelerated Cost Recovery System" and "Depreciation."

Accelerated Cost Recovery System (ACRS) A system provided under the Economic Recovery Tax Act of 1981 (ERTA) to determine deductions available on capital assets such as real estate; includes straight-line depreciation as well as accelerated cost recovery. See "Depreciation" and pages 9 and 11-18.

After-Tax The effective cost of, or return from, an investment, taking into consideration the tax effects. Pages 19, 30, and 50.

All-Inclusive Promissory Note See "Wraparound Mortgage" and pages 25-30.

Amortization (Loan) The reduction of debt (and resultant increase in equity) via regularly scheduled principal payments over the length of the loan term. Pages 4, 17-18, and 46.

Balloon Payment A payment on a note, on or before the debt's maturity, which is greater than a normal payment on the note; generally, the final payment. Pages 22 and 59.

Capital Gains Economic gains on investments subject to a more favorable federal tax rate. In real estate, capital gains can be maintained on eligible appreciation and on varying amounts of the gain attributable to depreciation or cost recovery deductions. Pages 4, 10, 25, and 29-30.

Capitalization Rate ("Cap Rate") A method of evaluating property which uses an analysis of the property's income and expenses, allowing for a vacancy factor. Pages 34-35, 37-41, and 46.

Cost Recovery A system of depreciation created by ERTA. See "Depreciation," "Accelerated Cost Recovery System," and pages 9-18.

Depreciation An accounting method that allows for the gradual loss of a capital asset's value by permitting annual deductions through the cost recovery period of the capital asset. See "ACRS," "Cost Recovery," and pages 8-9, 15, and 17-18.

Double Taxation Income taxation both at the business entity level and the investor level; for example, in some corporate forms, income is taxed when received by the corporation and again when passed through to investors as dividends. Income from partnerships and most income from real estate investment trusts, however, is not taxed at the entity level, but only when distributed to investors. Page 63.

Equity The difference between the fair market value and the existing debt on a property. Pages 4, 17, 23, 25-30, 41, and 46.

General Partner(s) A partner with full management responsibility and unlimited liability for the debts of the partnership; in a limited partnership, usually also the sponsor. See "General Partnership," "Limited Partnership," and pages 56 and 60.

(continued)

7

Appendix

75

General Partnership   An entity whose partners are jointly and severally liable for partnership obligations. Page 60.

Gross Multiplier   A method of evaluating property which uses an analysis of the property's income, compared to that of similar properties in the same or comparable market area. Pages 34-37, and 52.

Leverage   The use of borrowed money (debt) in relation to equity; a highly leveraged real estate transaction carries a large percentage of financing. Pages 2, 4, 15, 19-22, 24, and 41.

Limited Partner(s)   Passive investors with limited liability in a limited partnership. See "Limited Partnership" and pages 55-62.

Limited Partnership   An entity whose partners are one or more general partners and one or more limited partners; records a Certificate of Limited Partnership with the proper authorities. Pages 22-23, 52, and 55-62.

Phantom Income   Taxable income without cash income; created at the point where taxable income exceeds cash distributed. Page 18.

Principal Payments   Regular payments to reduce the non-interest portion of a mortgage. Pages 4, 8, 11-18, and 22.

Purchase Money Financing   See "Wraparound Mortgage" and pages 25-30.

Real Estate Investment Trust (REIT)   A business organization investing in equity and/or mortgages on properties and providing a flow-through of tax treatment of income (but not losses) to its shareholders; required to distribute a stipulated percentage of its earnings (ordinary income) to shareholders. Pages 22-23, 58, 60, and 63.

Replacement Cost   The cost of replacing a property with one of the same earning power. Pages 2, 34, and 49.

Reproduction Cost   The cost of reproducing a like property in the same location.

Self-Liquidating Program   An investment vehicle which, at inception, provides for liquidation and distribution of assets at a future date; for example, public real estate limited partnerships provide for a limited life in organizational documents. Pages 61-63.

Sponsor   Organizer and/or manager of an investment program, or one who participates in the management. Pages 30, 56-59, and 65-70.

Sub-Chapter S Corporation ("S" Corporation)   A corporation electing to be taxed as a partnership (allowing the flow-through of tax consequences to the owners as partners). Page 60.

Syndication   A group of persons or concerns who combine their funds, efforts, and expertise to make an investment; as used in real estate, commonly involves investors who pool their capital under the management of a sponsor/general partner. Pages vi, 30, and 55-70.

Tax-Sheltered Program   A pooled investment from which participants receive a "flow-through" of investment benefits and tax consequences, thereby reducing taxable income. Pages vi, 53, and 61-63.

Wraparound Mortgage   Used in refinancing property, the face amount of the "wrap" includes equity of the lender, plus the balance of the underlying loan(s); borrower makes all-inclusive payments. The holder of the wrap (the lender) then makes the payment(s) on the underlying loan(s). Pages 25-30.

PROFILES

Alan J. Parisse, SRS *

Alan J. Parisse is a nationally recognized real estate consultant, real estate broker, and syndicator. He is the president of Mill-Park Consultants Inc., New York, and is affiliated with Consolidated Capital Communications Group, Inc. (CCCG).

The 1983 president of the Real Estate Securities and Syndication Institute (RESSI) of the National Association of Realtors (NAR) and a long-standing member of its Executive Committee, Mr. Parisse is also a member of the Real Estate Committee of the National Association of Securities Dealers (NASD).

A leading speaker on real estate and other tax-advantaged investments, Mr. Parisse has trained more than 20,000 professionals. He has served as a consultant to numerous companies, including Connecticut General Life Insurance Company (now CIGNA). In addition, he is a senior instructor for RESSI and NAR and has been the featured speaker on syndication at the NAR's annual convention for the past eight years. Mr. Parisse has also instructed the staff of the NASD on real estate and tax-advantaged investments.

Mr. Parisse is well known for his widely selling audio cassette program on real estate syndication and has also written numerous articles and several books, including **How to Syndicate Real Estate** and **Financial Analysis of a Real Estate Investment**. With Richard G. Wollack, he co-authored **Tax-Advantaged Investments,** a widely utilized self-study program in tax shelters published by CCCG.

*SRS—Specialist in Real Estate Securities, the professional designation of the Real Estate Securities and Syndication Institute (RESSI)

Mr. Parisse has served as senior vice president of Oppenheimer Properties, the real estate affiliate of Oppenheimer and Company, Inc., a member of the New York Stock Exchange. He has been instrumental in the syndication and management of real properties valued in excess of $100 million.

A graduate of the University of Buffalo with a B.S. degree, Mr. Parisse was elected to the national honorary business fraternity Beta Gamma Sigma while attaining an M.B.A. from the University of Arizona.

Richard G. Wollack, SRS*

Richard G. Wollack, leader in the real estate syndication industry and nationally known author and lecturer on real estate investing and securities matters, is executive vice president of the Consolidated Capital companies, the nation's largest real estate syndication firm. Also president of an affiliated firm, Consolidated Capital Institutional Advisors, Inc., he was instrumental in forming Consolidated Capital Institutional Properties, a $200 million public limited partnership designed exclusively for tax-exempt investors.

Mr. Wollack, who began his real estate career more than 12 years ago as co-founder and president of the Florida-based First Capital Companies, ran a national real estate investment consulting firm bearing his name before he joined Consolidated Capital in 1981. A specialist in due diligence procedures for broker dealer firms and investment analysis of real estate sponsors and programs, Mr. Wollack is a frequent contributor to national real estate and financial periodicals, including a regular column for **Wealthbuilding** (formerly **National Tax Shelter Digest**), and regular contributions to the **Real Estate Securities Journal,** of which he is a member of the editorial advisory board.

(continued)

<u>Tax-Advantaged Investments,</u> the widely utilized self-study program in tax shelters published by Consolidated Capital Communications Group, Inc. (CCCG), was co-authored by Alan Parisse and Mr. Wollack.

A principal and financial principal of the National Association of Securities Dealers, a member of the national board of the International Association for Financial Planning, and a member of both the Western Pension Conference and Pension Realty Advisors, Mr. Wollack has been an instructor for the Real Estate Securities and Syndication Institute of the National Association of Realtors.

He received an M.B.A. with distinction from the Stanford University Graduate School of Business in 1969 after being graduated Phi Beta Kappa from the University of Illinois two years previously. For the past three years, he has co-chaired the prestigious Stanford Real Estate Symposium, an annual conference featuring series of presentations by economists and prominent real estate professionals.

Joyce G. Harold

Joyce G. Harold, special publications director of the Consolidated Capital companies, supervised the compilation of materials and the production of <u>The Real Estate Investment Pocket Guide.</u>

Since joining Consolidated Capital in 1975, Ms. Harold has authored and edited numerous articles and volumes on investment real estate, limited partnerships, and real estate investment trusts for the firm. Currently in charge of market communications for the firm's field offices, she also works closely with CCCG, publishers of <u>The Real Estate Investment Pocket Guide,</u> in its activities for the investment community. Formerly, she was advertising director and corporate communications director for the firm.

A 1969 graduate of the University of Missouri School of Journalism with a specialty in magazines, Ms. Harold began her career on Midwestern newspapers and subsequently was on the national editorial magazine staff of Triangle Publications. A member of Women in Communications, Inc. and a former national membership committee member, she is an accredited member of the International Association of Business Communicators.

ACKNOWLEDGEMENTS

A number of individuals made contributions to this volume, and we want especially to thank Linda Lazare of Consolidated Capital, who contributed pre-publication research and ideas. Others at Consolidated Capital who made significant contributions to this volume were the following: Dora Lew, James Miller, and Vicki Lateano.

The authors also wish to thank R.A. Stanger & Co., Fair Haven, New Jersey, for research materials.

Illustrations: Frank Ansley, San Francisco, California
Graphic Design & Production: Larry Westdal and Victor Ichioka, San Francisco, California
Typesetting: Mercury Typography, San Francisco, California
Printing: Trans Forms, Inc., San Rafael, California
Binding: Moffitt's Bindery Service, Petaluma, California
Distribution: Under the auspices of Consolidated Capital Communications Group, Inc.

7

Appendix

Notes

Notes

KNOW YOUR TAX SHELTERS

Now, you don't have to be a financial wizard to understand the complex world of tax-shelter investing.

Tax-Advantaged Investments, published by Consolidated Capital Communications Group, Inc., does almost all the work for you. Co-authors Alan Parisse and Richard Wollack, the same team that authored *The Real Estate Investment Pocket Guide,* combined 25 years of experience in the tax-shelter field to give you nearly 400 pages on topics such as "Life Cycle of a TAI", "Oil & Gas", "Real Estate", "Federal Securities Regulations", and "Taxation", all keyed to cassette recordings.

Tax-Advantaged Investments also is a comprehensive study guide for the NASD Series 22 examination—in other words, a complete dual-purpose tool for licensing as well as for sales training.

Noted tax-shelter expert Robert A. Stanger says: "It's one of the best basic compilations of material I've seen in the tax-shelter area."

BUSINESS REPLY MAIL
FIRST CLASS PERMIT NO. 5593 OAKLAND, CA

POSTAGE WILL BE PAID BY ADDRESSEE

**Consolidated Capital
Communications Group, Inc.**
1900 Powell Street, Suite 1000
Emeryville, CA 94608

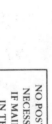